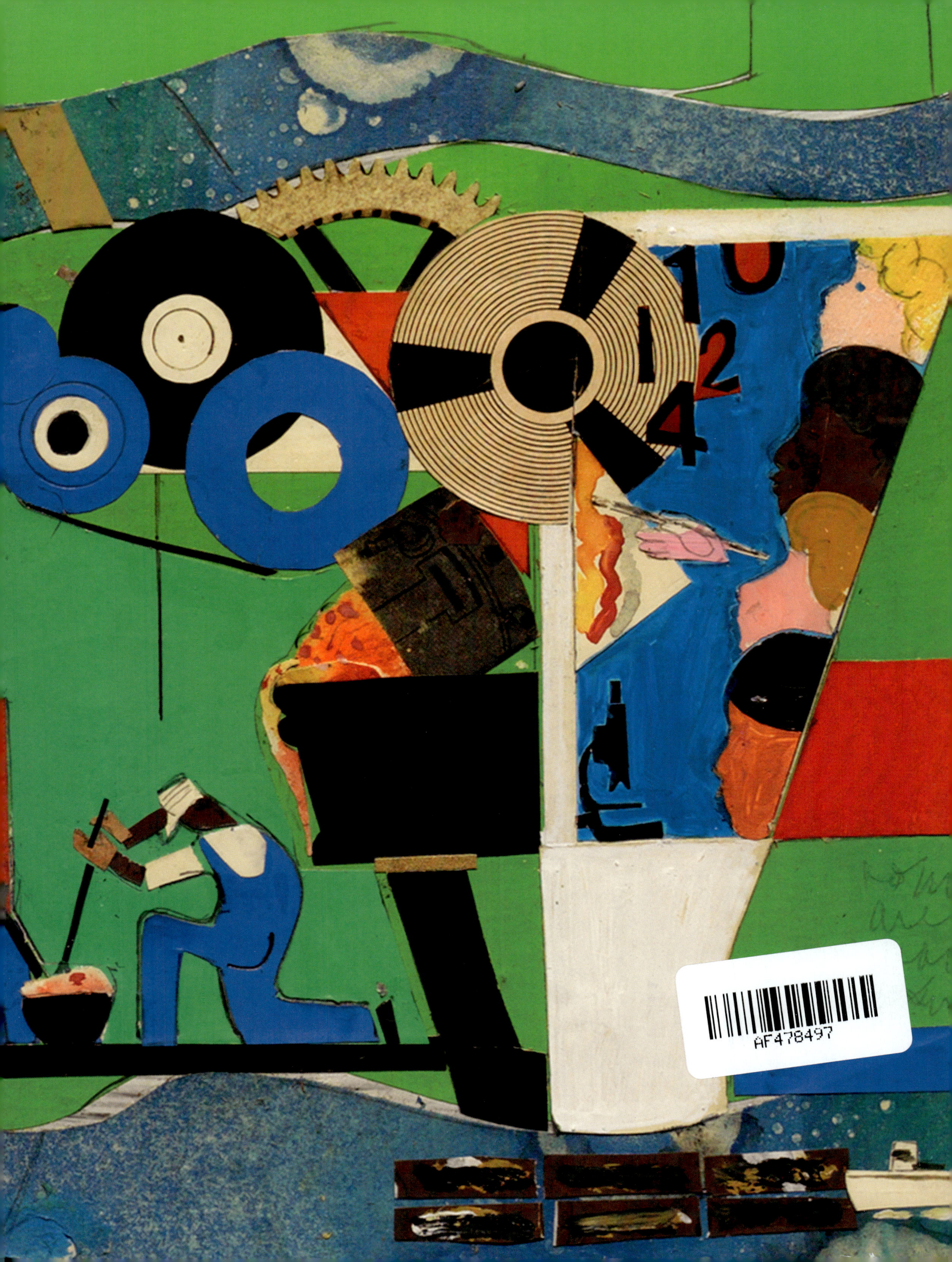
AF478497

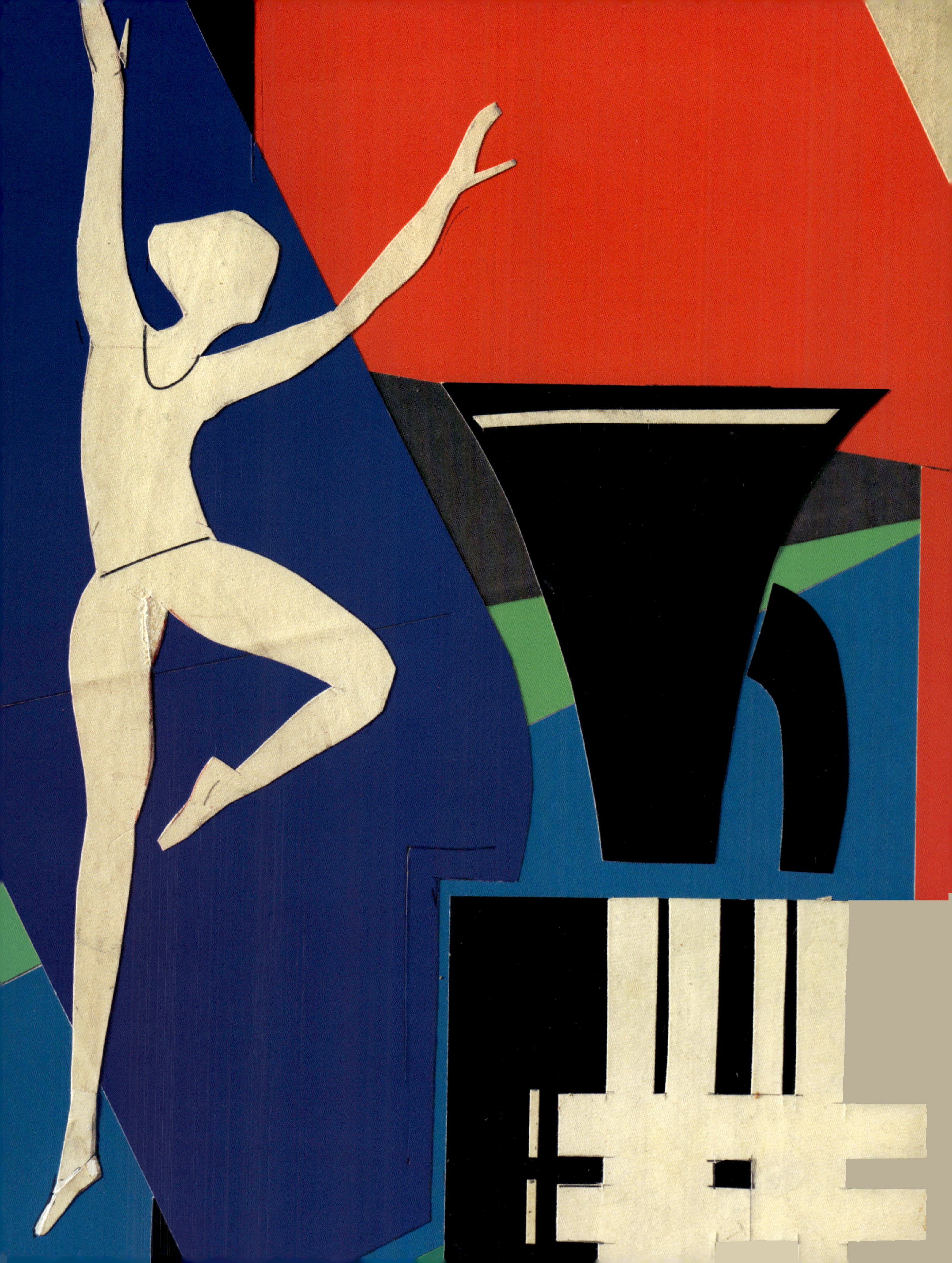

# ROMARE
# BEARDEN

*Idea to Realization*

Essay by Sarah E. Lewis

DC**MOORE** GALLERY

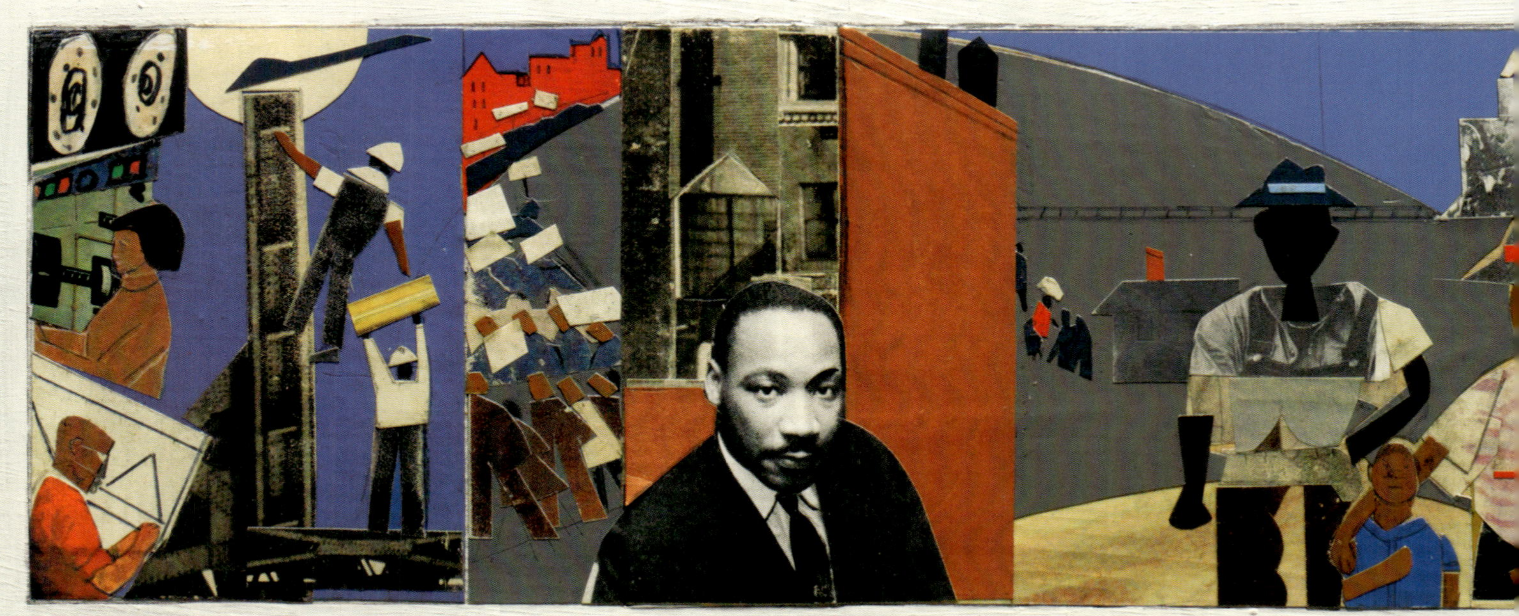



A SYMBOLIC PAGEANT OF AFRO-AMERICAN HISTORY, 1972. COLLAGE ON FIBERBOARD, 6 X 26 INCHES

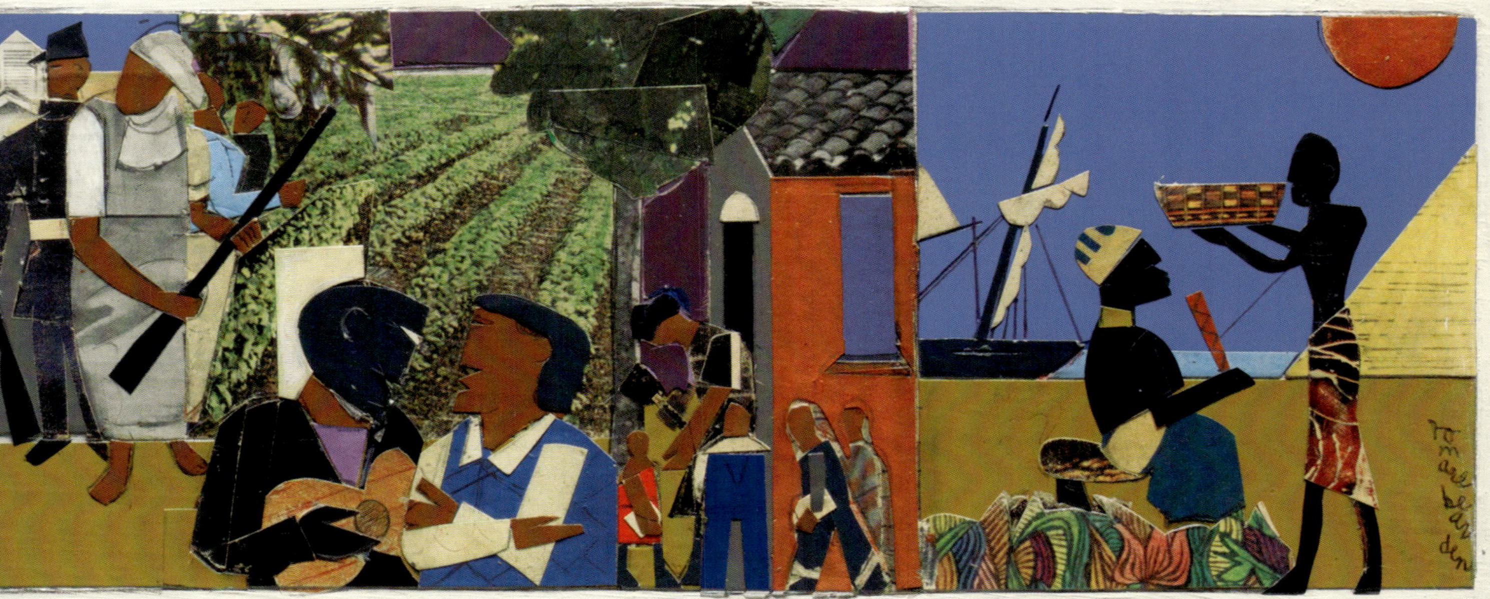



THE RURAL SCENE

THE AFRICAN HERITAGE

# NEW ENCOUNTERS

*Sarah E. Lewis*

**THROUGHOUT THE AGES**, artists have been truth tellers for our civilizations; they speak about the essence of their society in ways that others cannot or will not. Some such artists have incantatory vision. Romare Bearden was endowed with this gift. In his hands, slashes of textures and color became so active that they could show a complete world and its development across time; his collaged and painted images could inspire a vision of who we might become and remind us of who we had been all along. So well known is his salutary oeuvre that it is hard to imagine coming upon sterling pieces for the first time as we do in the exhibition *Romare Bearden: Idea to Realization*. These infrequently seen maquettes for murals, mosaics, and book projects give us a rare glimpse into the creative endeavor of this "Ellington of twentieth-century painters" from conceptualization to completion.[1]

Bearden's process was punctuated by formative, often private encounters. Viewing the maquettes in this exhibition—pieces perhaps seen in the studio only by friends and family—puts us in their company. The poet Elizabeth Alexander described how, as a college student writing a paper, she rang up Bearden, having found his number in the phone book. He spoke to her at length about his creative process. "By the end of the conversation he had sent me to Sun Tzu's *The Art of War*, any stained glass windows I could find," she said, "and Earl 'Fatha' Hines's music, so that I might better understand his own work."[2] Bearden's working method integrated his uncommon gift for connection, communication, and mentorship; more still recall how they found encouragement in going to Bearden's 125th Street and later Canal Street Studios, which became institutions, as it were, such that they warranted a capital S. The interests that guided his work connected him to the litany of artists who considered Bearden a friend. For Ralph Ellison, who recalls going to his 125th Street Studio, it forged their love of "folktales;" their "shared ancestral lore made for a level of unspoken communication which connected the past to the present."[3]

"I've discovered that I work essentially in collage," said playwright August Wilson, who first encountered *The Prevalence of Ritual* in 1977.[4] "Being an admirer of Romare Bearden's collages, I try to make my plays the equal of his canvases."[5] The Pittsburgh native mentioned the impress that Bearden has had on his work in this way: "My influences have been what I call my four Bs— the primary one being the blues, then Borges, Baraka, and Bearden." Bearden once told Wilson, "I try and explore, in terms of the life I know best, those things which are common to all cultures." It was a method that Wilson employed as well, using language he recalled from growing up in Pittsburgh; for example, hanging around Pat's Place, a cigar store turned community spot, gave him stories that would make their way into Wilson's *Ma Rainey's Black Bottom*. "Through Bearden, I realized that you could arrive at the universal through the specific," Wilson said. It was a practice that made the artist's work both topical and timeless.[6]

From his earliest stages, Bearden's talent inspired others, even from afar. An encounter with his work was likely what moved James Thrall Soby, then Director of the Armed Services Program at The Museum of Modern Art, on November 16, 1944, to write a letter to Major Leo Friedman about "Sgt. Bearden." Soby hoped that "in his leisure time he could paint mural decorations which would be of great interest to military personnel and civilians alike."[7] But Bearden wasn't interested in making murals at that time, as he explained to Myron Schwartzman, "I was just trying how to paint a bit, in the forties!"[8] His murals would come nearly thirty years later, but from Bearden's nascent stages, his work declaimed the need to honor African American culture and it became of inestimable value to a broad audience, as Soby felt it might.

The importance of valuing African American culture as a contribution to our collective heritage was central to Bearden's artistic mission and a point that he made while moderating the symposium, "The Black Artist in

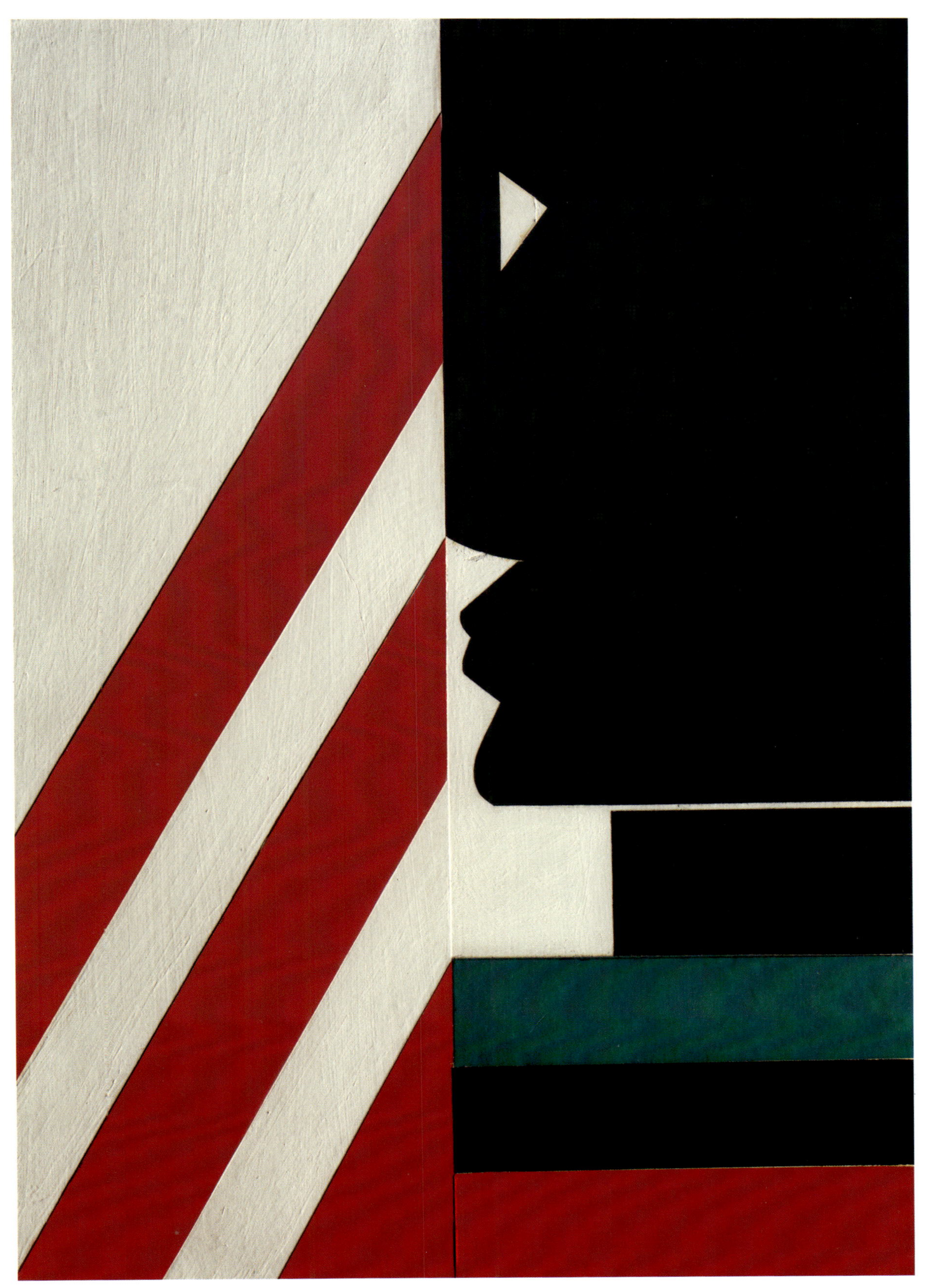

GENEVA PRINT MAQUETTE, 1971. COLLAGE ON PLYWOOD, 20 X 14 3/8 INCHES

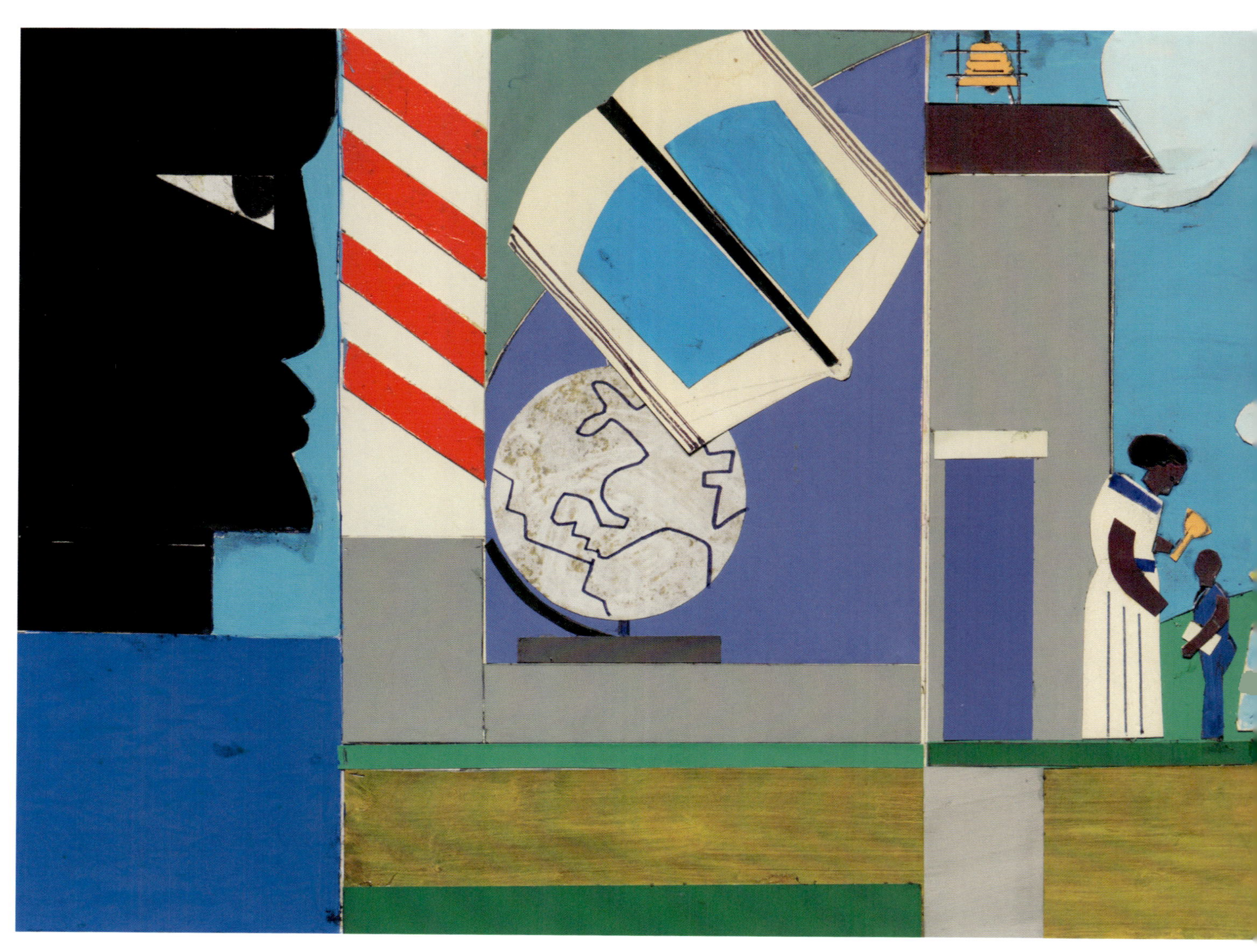

 **BLACK HISTORY**, c.1979. COLLAGE ON ILLUSTRATION BOARD, 9 X 26 INCHES

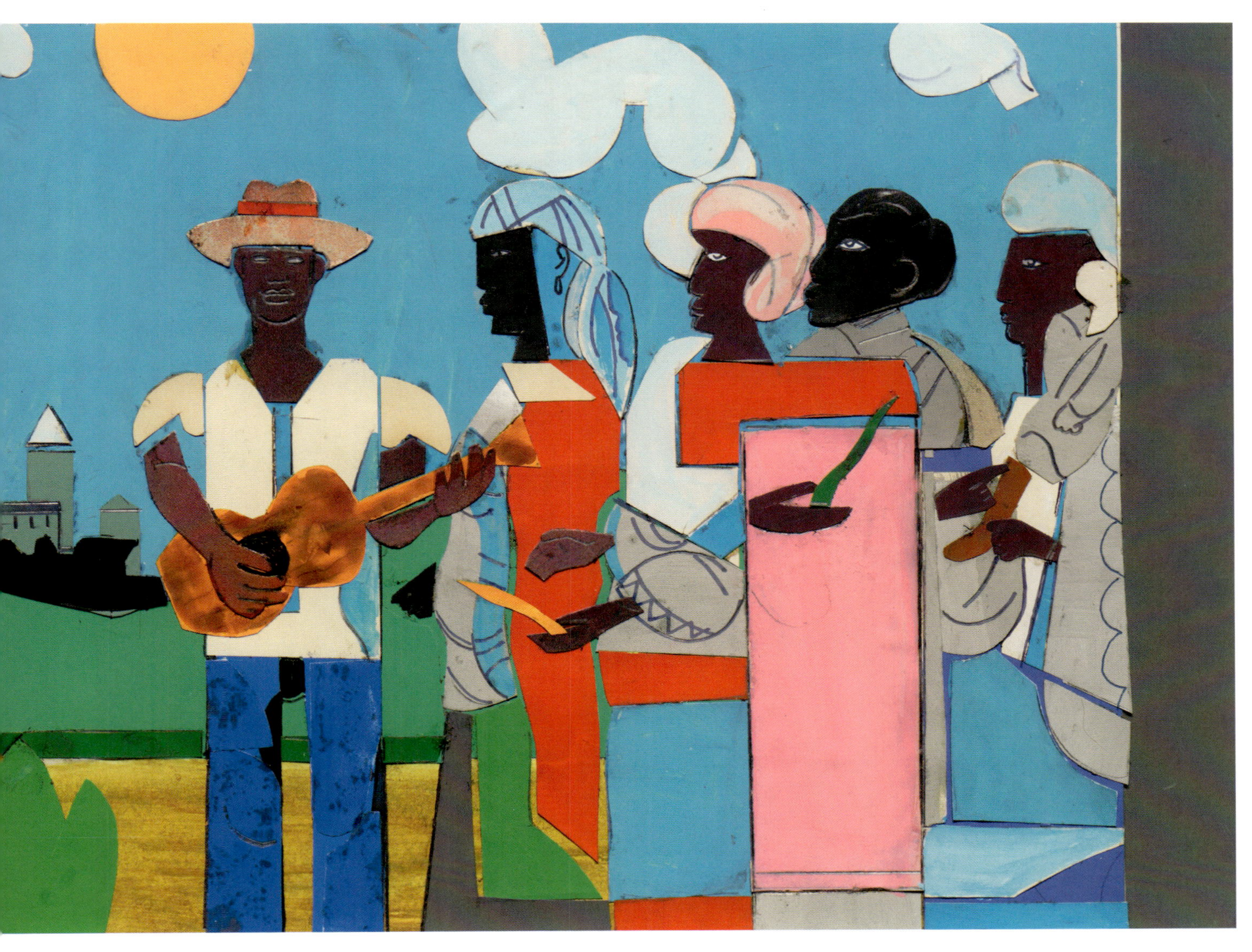

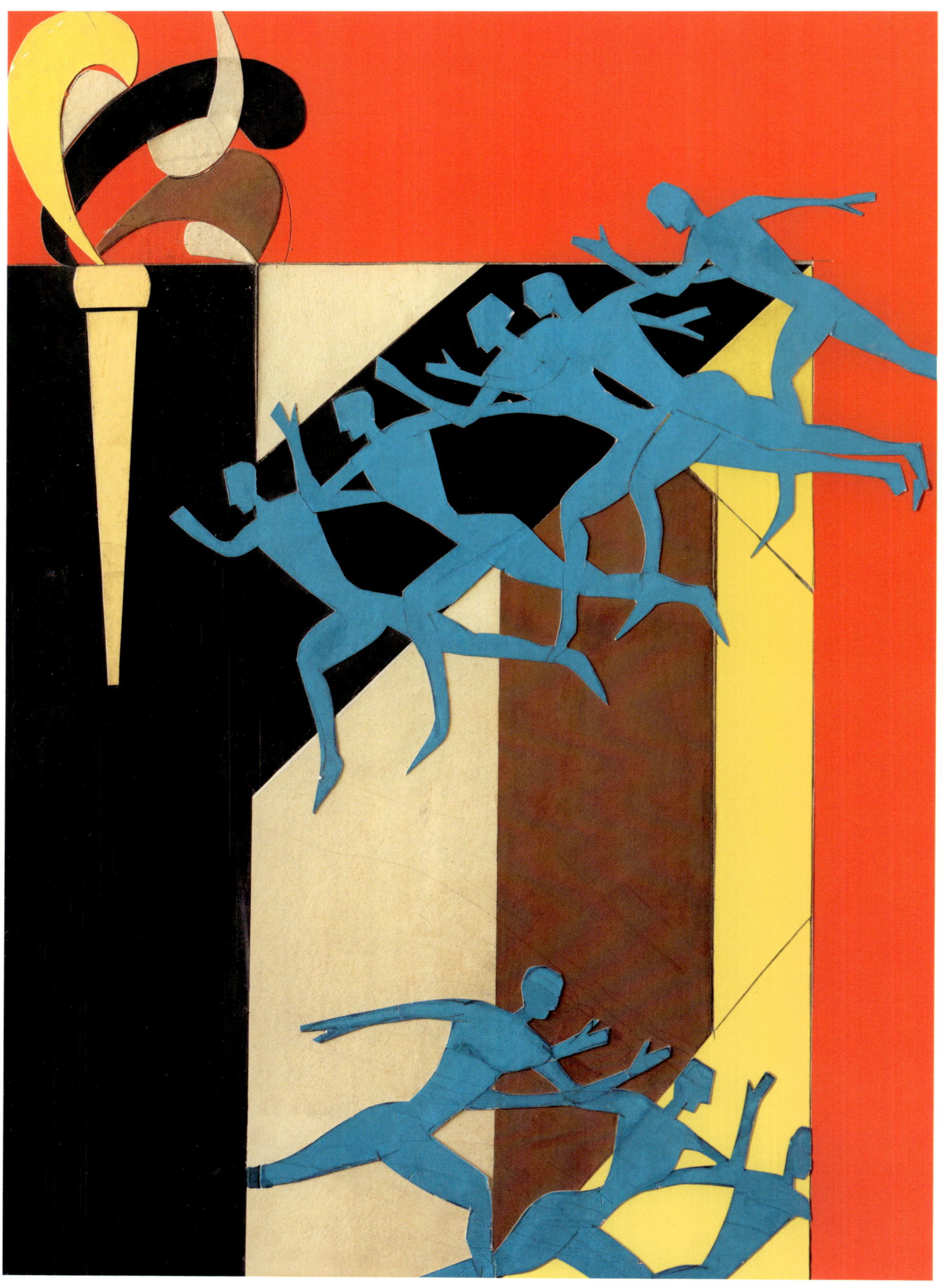

10    OLYMPICS POSTER MAQUETTE, 1975. COLLAGE ON FIBERBOARD, 15$\frac{1}{8}$ X 11$\frac{1}{8}$ INCHES

America," held at The Metropolitan Museum of Art in 1969. The panel featured Sam Gilliam, Jr., Richard Hunt, Jacob Lawrence, Tom Lloyd, William Williams, and Hale Woodruff. Bearden interrupted his role as moderator to emphasize this point:

> They say that abstract expressionism—action paint-ing—is the first indigenous American art exported, and imitated by artists all around the world. No critic that I have read has ever aligned this spark with jazz music. But that's the feeling you get from it: involve-ment, personality, improvisation, rhythm, color. What I'm trying to point out is that Black culture is involved far more into the whole cultural fabric of American life than we realize. But it is up to us to find out the con-tribution that we have made to the whole cultural fabric of American life. No one else is going to do it.[9]

Bearden's words spoke as forcefully as his work. His deci-sion to move from painting to collage allowed him "to look at anything in my encounters with the outside that might help translate the innerness of the Negro experience."[10] It led to the feat of "conjoining diverse and divergent bits of life into a unified expression."[11]

His maquette for what remains to date an unknown project, *A Symbolic Pageant of Afro-American History* (1972), exemplifies the extent of his encyclopedic focus on African American heritage and culture. Central to this potent four-paneled collage is the image of Martin Luther King, Jr., unmanipulated save for three black paint marks—one following the thickening line of his eyebrow, the other two under his shirt collar—trans-forming the figure into a historical bust. After King's assassination, an aesthetic that used the longitude of spread in a scrolled format recapitulated the develop-ment of African American culture—both in artistic works and in exhibitions themselves beginning in 1969. For some, this spread became an act of *memento mori*, occur-ring as it did after King's murder. But in Bearden's hands,

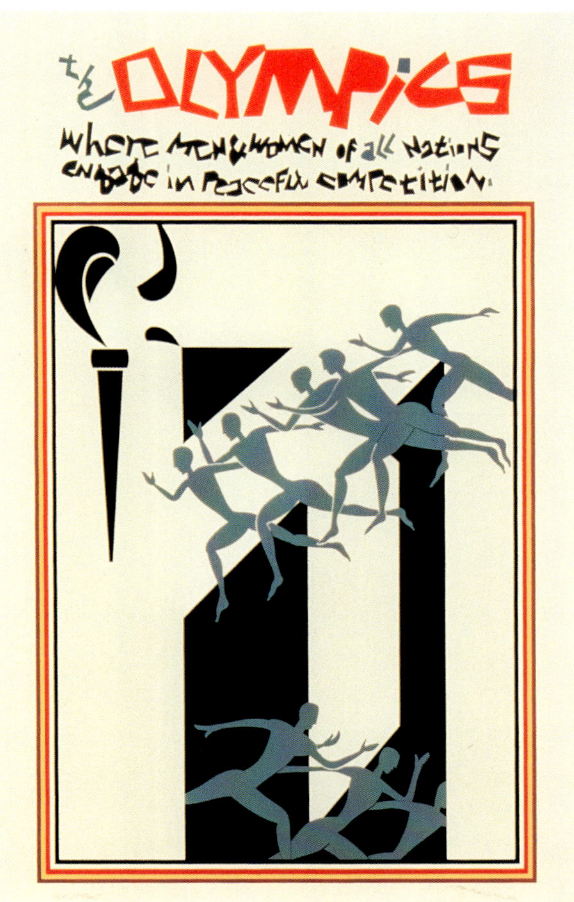



Romare Bearden: *Olympics Poster*, 1976. 39 x 25 inches.

his own aesthetic unfurling had the tone of a New Orleans funeral parade; King is first laid to rest and the piece goes on as a celebration of African diasporic culture.

Bearden's tonally restrained maquette for the cover of *Poems from Africa* (1973), a volume edited by Samuel Allen, is built on his deep engagement with African her-itage. His figurative silhouetted focus evokes African masking traditions coupled with the "off-beat phrasing," as Robert Farris Thompson terms it, of Mande textiles suggested by the skewed patterned background lines.[12] When his visual vocabulary was more communicative than compositional, when it was designed to indicate more than declaim, it still conveyed his signature style with deliberately paired down details that emphasized unmistakable bold forms.

Bearden's work was also engaged with encounters of the more spiritual kind; conjure was the foundation of his creative process (whether or not this tradition was the particular subject of that work). As acts of conjure, each of his works operates as a conjunction, suturing together the seeming separation among people through sound, sight, and touch. His *Pittsburgh Recollections* (1984), one of the last of his public works for a subway station in Pittsburgh, offers an elegant scroll about the development of the city and its citizens. Other works in Bearden's Pittsburgh series, inspired by his experience, are also composed of other influences—as in the case of *The Twenties: Pittsburgh Memories, Farewell Eugene* (1978), which evokes Giotto's compositions as well as Italian Renaissance painter, Duccio's work. The result is that Bearden's art draws from and speaks across ages.

How do you convey what cannot be contained? Bearden did so with deft skill in *Bessie, Duke, and Louis* (c. 1981), which is related to an unrealized book project with Albert Murray and Sam Shaw. His extended horizontal piece takes on the elongated form of a scroll with piano keys where words might be. For Bearden—as with the musicians Bessie, Duke, and Louis—the key was improvisation. His sense of the importance of music and sound extended to his exhibitions and comments about his own craft, both in terms of his process and the nature of creativity itself.

"In essence, art is an old tune that the artist plays with new variations," Bearden was known to say. One of Bearden's friends, jazz musician Wynton Marsalis recently asked, "A financial inheritance can be accurately assessed in dollars, but what is the value of an artistic heritage? Who calculates the value of 'Amazing Grace' or 'Yankee Doodle' or 'Go Down Moses'?"[13] Bearden was asking similar questions of African American culture. Through an alchemical creative process, he dared to ask how we honor and perpetuate culture and in so doing created works of timeless and incalculable value.

**HISTORIAN, WRITER, AND CURATOR SARAH E. LEWIS** received her B.A. from Harvard University, an M.Phil from Oxford University, and is nearing completion on her doctoral dissertation at Yale University. Cocurator of the 2010 SITE Santa Fe Biennial, she was selected as a member of President Obama's Arts Policy Committee and is on the board of The Andy Warhol Foundation for the Visual Arts. Her book *RISE: The Power of Failure in Pursuit of Success*, drawing on her work in the visual arts and expanding into sports, business, psychology, sociology, and science to explore the importance of so called failure in human endeavor, will be published by Simon & Schuster (U.S.), HarperCollins (U.K.).


1. Robert G. O'Meally, "Romare Bearden's Black Odyssey: A Search for Home," in *Romare Bearden: A Black Odyssey*, exh. cat. (New York: DC Moore Gallery, 2007), p. 10.

2. Elizabeth Alexander, "The Genius of Romare Bearden," *Power and Possibility: Essays, Reviews and Interviews*, (Ann Arbor: The University of Michigan Press, 2007), p. 34.

3. Ralph Ellison, "Bearden," *Callaloo*, No. 36 (Summer 1988), p. 417.

4. August Wilson, "August Wilson: The Art of Theater," *The Paris Review*, No. 153 (Winter 1999).

5. Ibid.

6. Ibid.

7. "Letter to Major Leo Friedman, November 16, 1944," James Thrall Soby Papers, The Museum of Modern Art Archives, New York.

8. Bearden quoted in Myron Schwartzman, *Romare Bearden: His Life and Art*, (New York: Abrams, 1990), p. 194.

9. Romare Bearden, Sam Gilliam, Jr., Richard Hunt, Jacob Lawrence, Tom Lloyd, William Williams, and Hale Woodruff, "The Black Artist in America: A Symposium," *The Metropolitan Museum of Art, New Series*, Vol. 27, No. 5 (1969), p. 254.

10. Richard J. Powell, "What Becomes a Legend Most?" *Transition*, No. 55 (1992), p. 66.

11. Ibid.

12. Robert Farris Thompson, *Flash of the Spirit* (New York: Vintage Books, 1983).

13. Wynton Marsalis, *The Ballad of the American Arts*, Nancy Hanks Lecture on Arts and Public Policy, The Kennedy Center, Washington D.C. March 31, 2009.

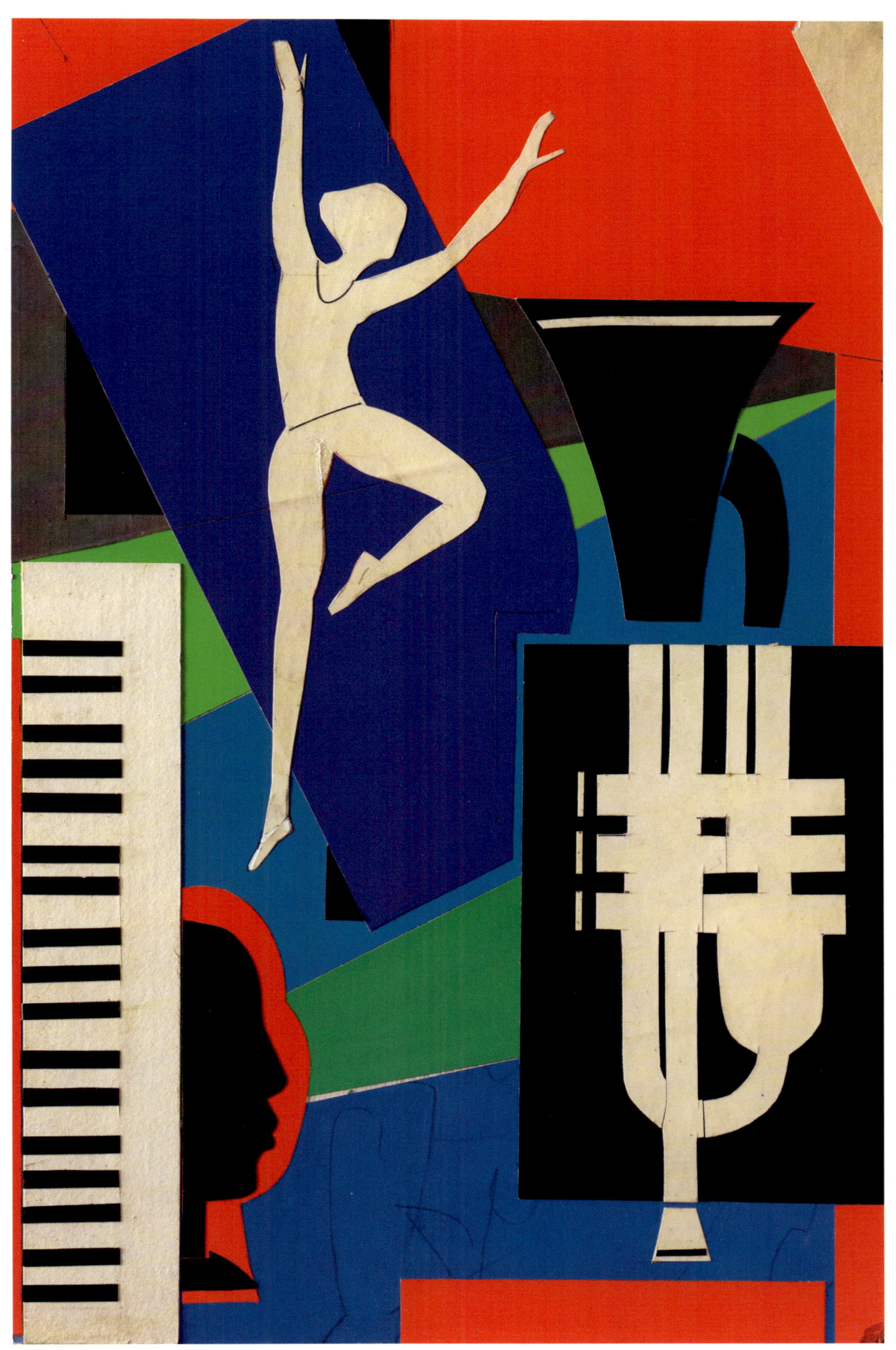

CULTURE: HARTFORD MURAL, 1980. COLLAGE ON FIBERBOARD, 18 X 12 INCHES

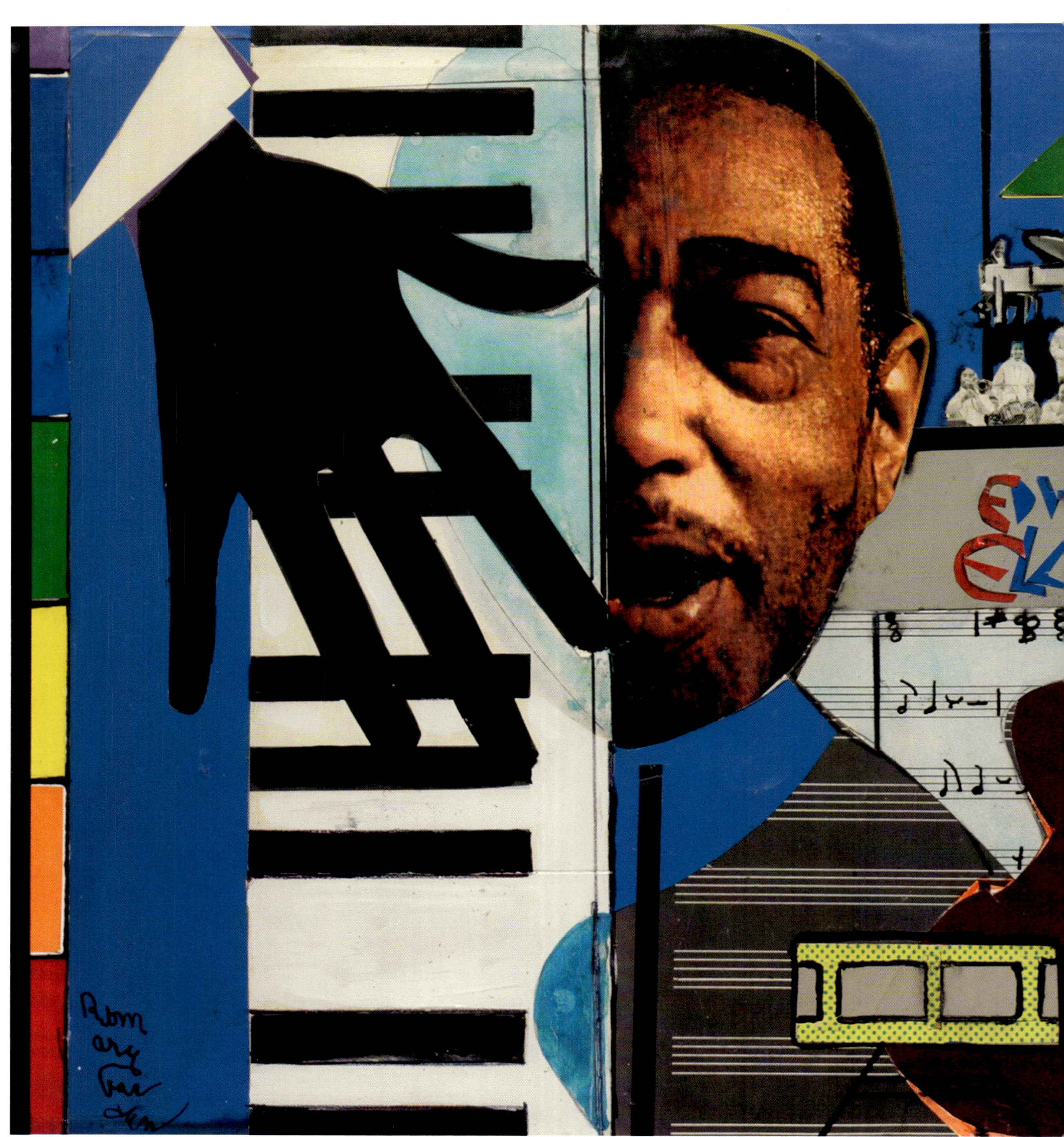

 BESSIE, DUKE, AND LOUIS, c. 1981. COLLAGE ON FIBERBOARD, 18 1/8 X 50 INCHES

# ON THE MAQUETTES

*Ralph Sessions*

## BESSIE, DUKE, AND LOUIS, c. 1981

**THROUGHOUT HIS CAREER,** Bearden collaborated with fellow artists, writers, musicians, and choreographers by creating artworks for books and designing book covers, posters, costumes, and stage sets. *Bessie, Duke, and Louis* is one example, a vibrant homage to these three jazz legends that is related to a book project conceived by Bearden and two close friends, Albert Murray, a novelist and jazz critic, and Sam Shaw, a photographer and film producer.

While the book was never realized, it inspired Bearden's *Jazz* series of 1981. The series was in turn prompted by some of Shaw's photographs and a 1961 film, *Paris Blues*, starring Paul Newman and Sidney Poitier as expatriate jazz musicians. Produced by Shaw, it is set in Paris in 1950, the same year that Bearden was there on the GI Bill. Louis Armstrong performed in the film, and Duke Ellington composed the musical score.

Shaw shot a large number of stills of Armstrong, Ellington, and band members on location in Paris in 1960 and 1961, some of which he made available to Bearden a few years later. The photos of Armstrong and Ellington in this collage are by Shaw, and the one of Bessie Smith may be as well, although the figure is largely a painterly construction.

Several of the works from the book project feature Ellington, such as *Ellington, Bill Strayhorn (Sacré-Coeur)* and *Ellington with Paris Graffiti*. Other evocative collages include *Casino de Paris*, *Cirque d'Hiver*, and *Paris Stairs*, as well as scenes set in Harlem, home of the Cotton Club, Savoy Ballroom, and Apollo Theatre in the 1930s and 1940s, and New Orleans, birthplace of Dixieland jazz.

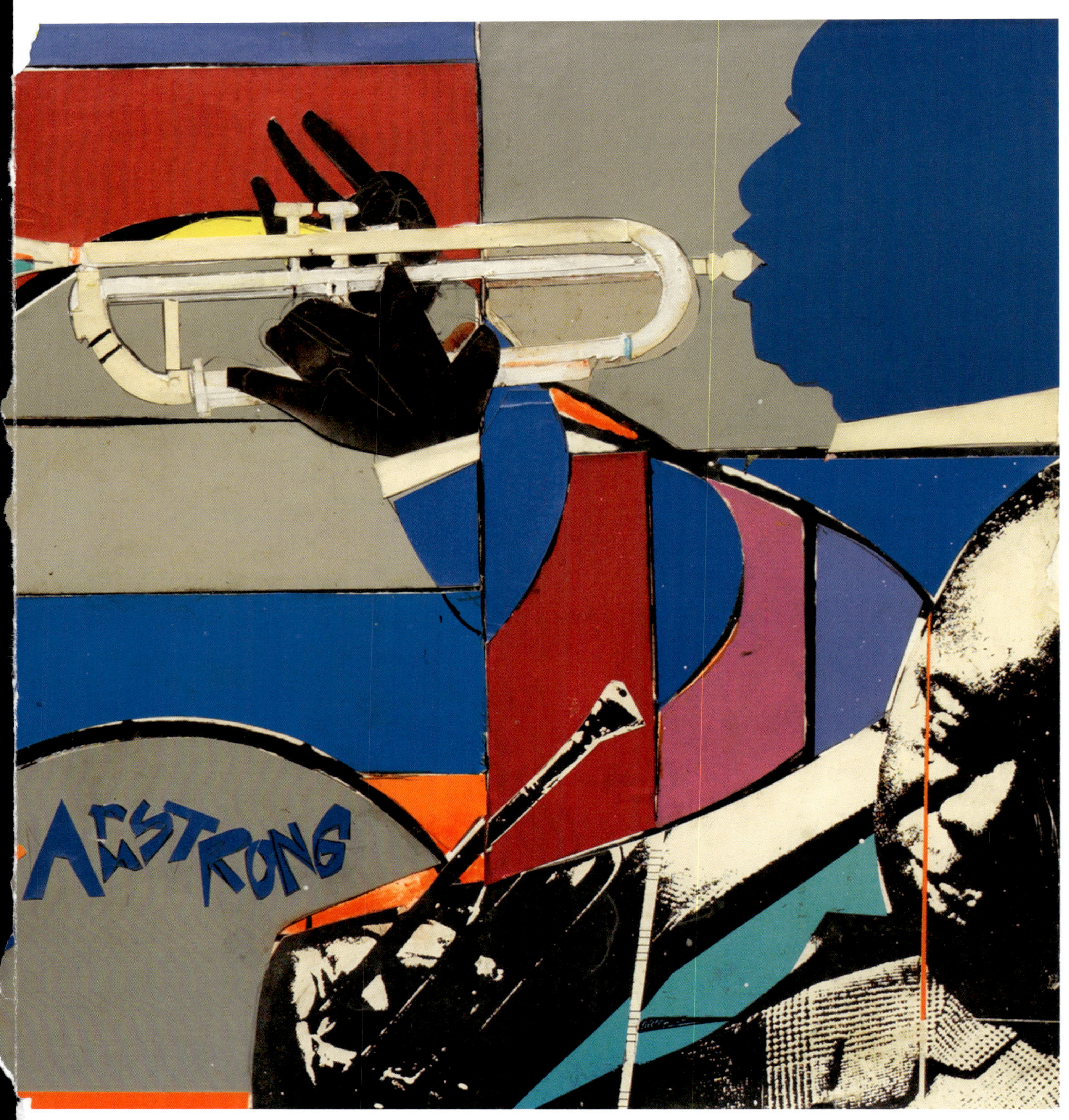
ARMSTRONG

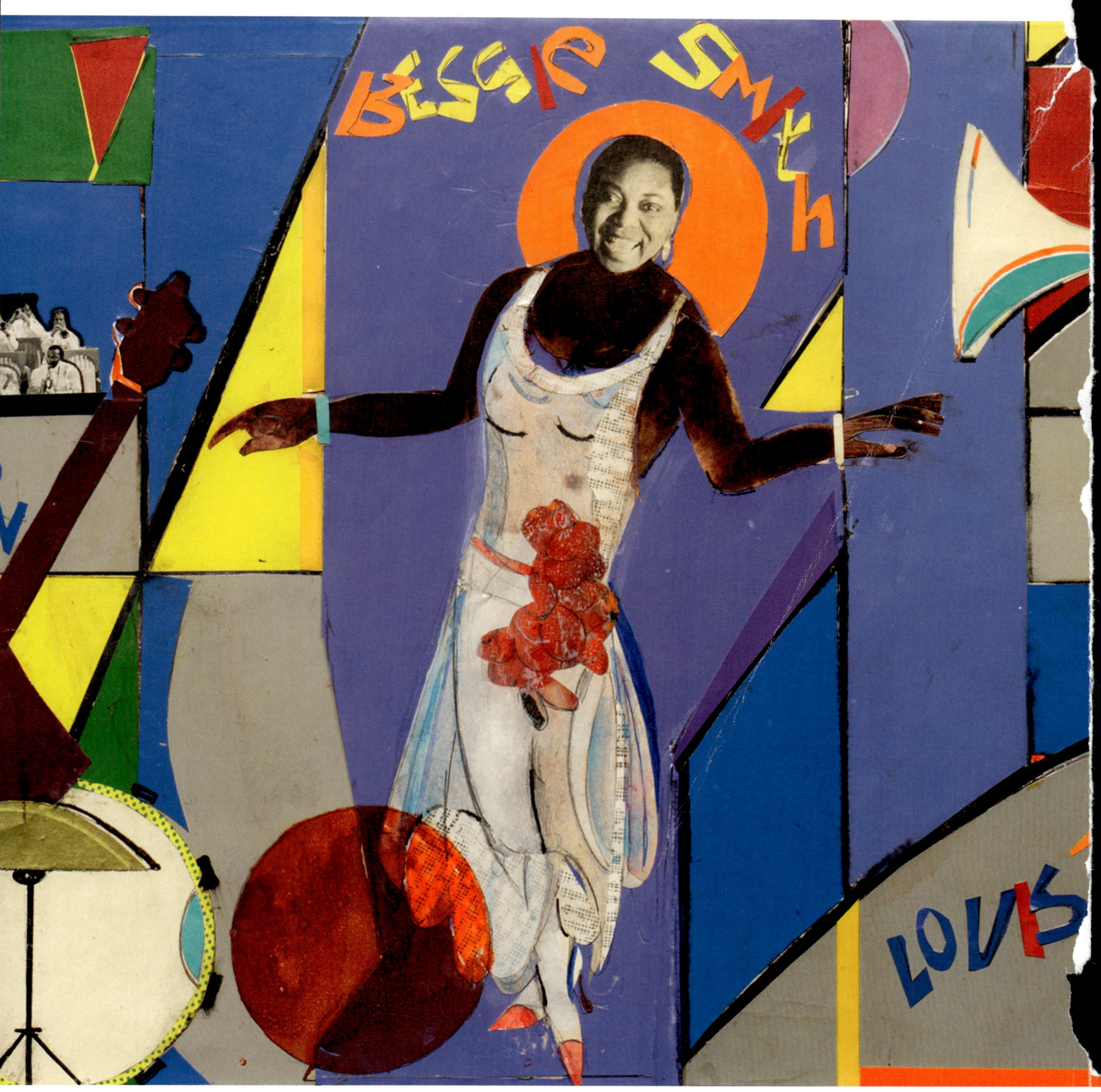

BESSIE SMITH
LOUIS

## SPORTS AND CULTURE: HARTFORD MURALS, 1980

**IN A 1980 INTERVIEW**, Bearden described this maquette and the one on page 13 as representing the "sports and the cultural aspect of Hartford." When he was commissioned for a project for the newly rebuilt Hartford Civic Center Coliseum in Connecticut, it was to be shared with the minimalist artist, Sol LeWitt, who was a native of the city.

LeWitt eventually withdrew his proposal due to a heated public controversy in which the appropriateness of his conceptualist work for the space was questioned by some city officials and local residents. Bearden at first resigned in sympathy with LeWitt, but subsequently responded by submitting designs for two canvas panels, 14 x 15 feet and 14 x 18 feet, which symbolize the sports and cultural events held at the coliseum. He intended that the athletic figure, half-black basketball player and half-white hockey player, express "a kind of unity" among the races that existed more in the world of sports than elsewhere in American society.

## A SYMBOLIC PAGEANT OF AFRO-AMERICAN HISTORY, 1972 *(pages 4/5)*

**THE AFRICAN AMERICAN EXPERIENCE** is concisely depicted in *A Symbolic Pageant of Afro-American History* in four panels labeled "The African Heritage," "The Rural Scene," "The Urban Crisis," and "Building the World of Tomorrow." The focal point is an image of Dr. Martin Luther King, Jr., a pivotal figure in modern history, surrounded by unnamed, representative characters that span the centuries.

Bracketed by images of ancient Egypt and African kingdoms on the right and the modern world of a computer technician and draftsman on the left, the central sections highlight principal themes of nineteenth and twentieth-century black life and the struggle for Civil Rights. By condensing each scene to its key elements, Bearden has heightened the power of a narrative that unfolds with the force of history.

Reflecting the powerful social currents of the time, the maquette also confirms Bearden's engagement with both personal artistic concerns and the tumultuous issues and events that surrounded him. As Ralph Ellison wrote in 1968,

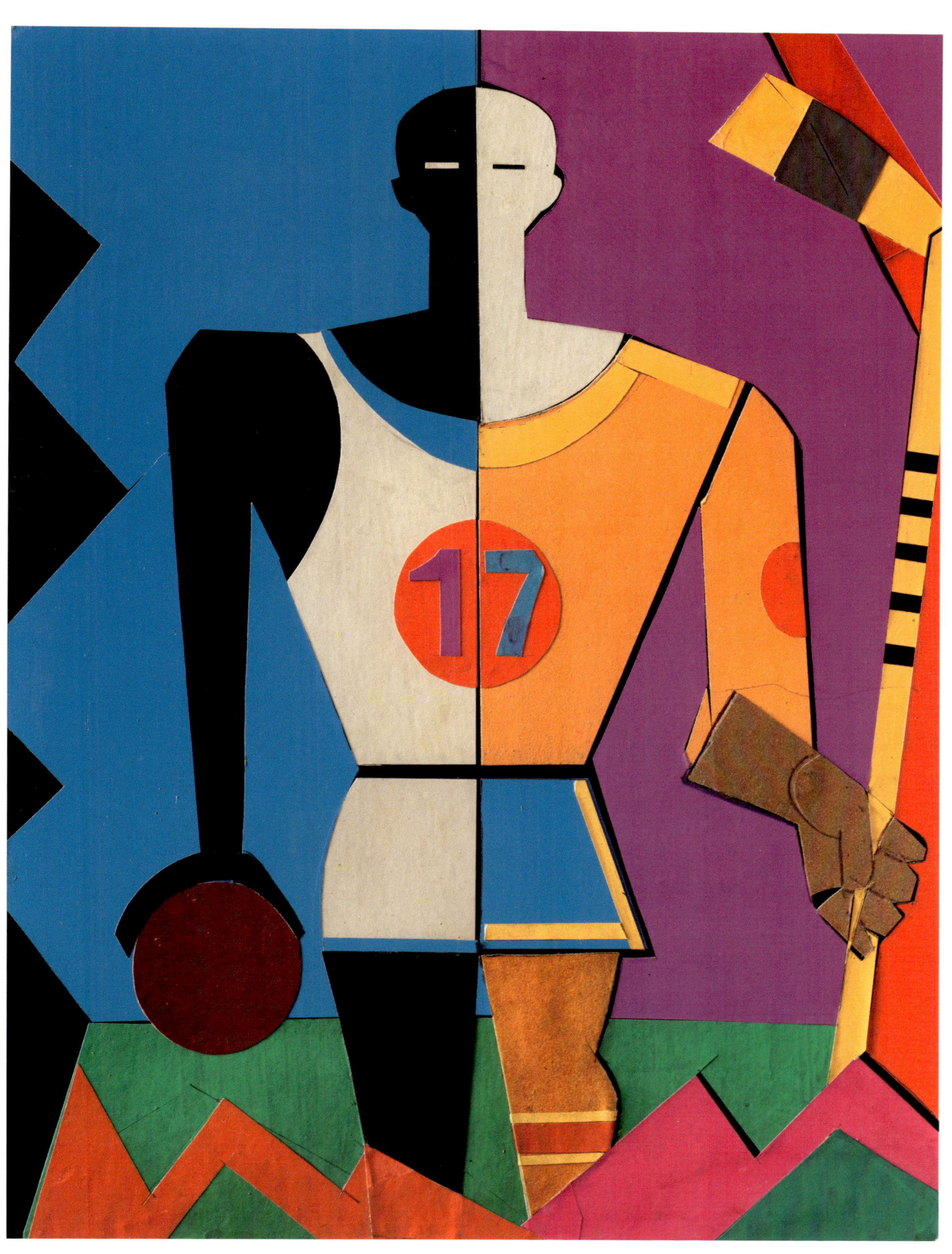

SPORTS: HARTFORD MURAL, 1980. COLLAGE ON FIBERBOARD, 18 X 14 INCHES

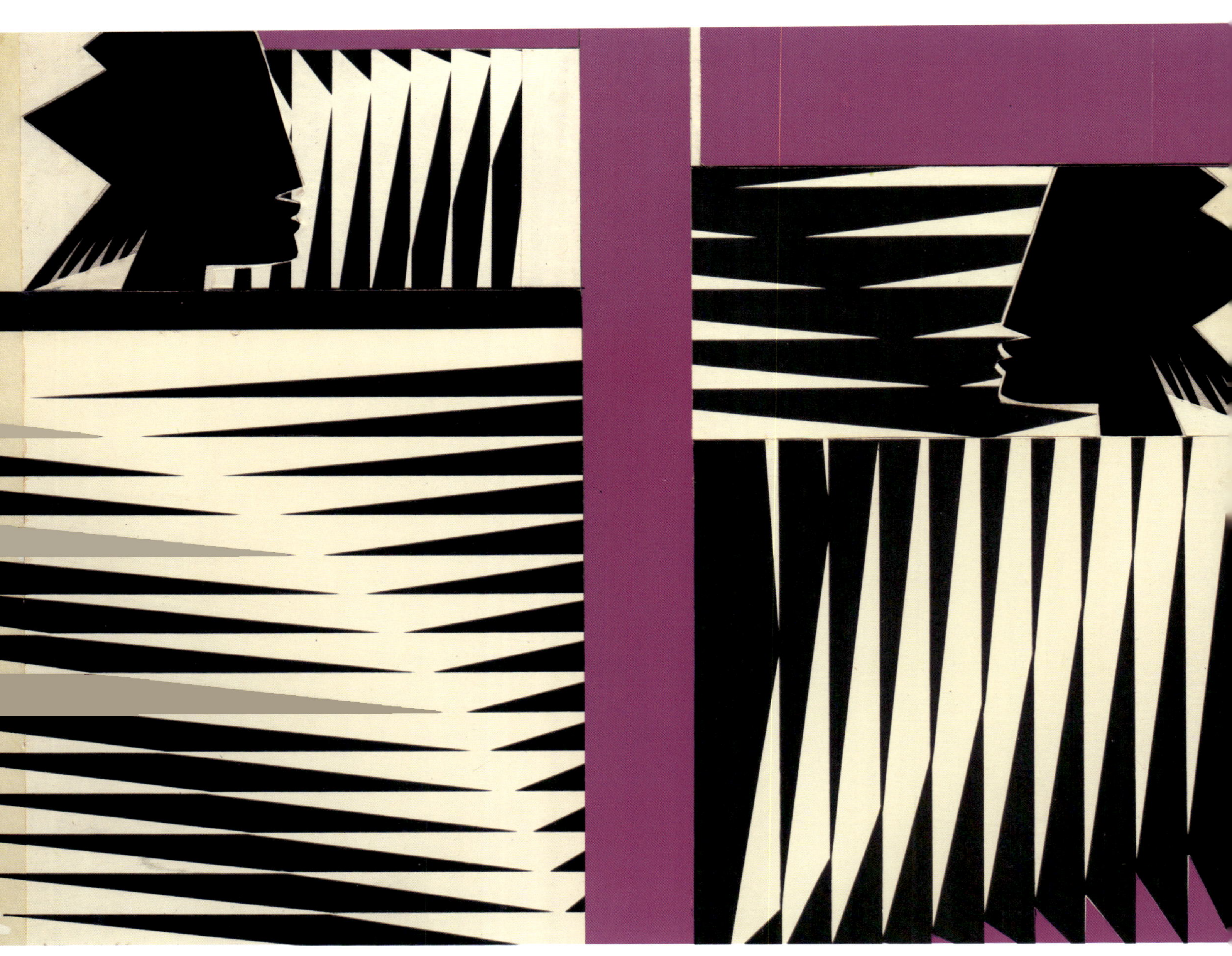

POEMS FROM AFRICA, 1973. COLLAGE ON FIBERBOARD, 14 X 20⅛ INCHES

Romare Bearden ... is an artist whose social consciousness is no less intense than his dedication to art; his example is of utmost importance for all who are concerned with grasping something of the complex interrelations between race, culture and the individual artist as they exist in the United States.[1]

1. Ralph Ellison, *Paintings and Projections* (Albany: Art Gallery, State University of New York, 1968).


## POEMS FROM AFRICA, 1973

**THE STRIKING DESIGN** of this maquette became a book cover for a collection of poems by African writers that was published in 1973. Bearden illustrated the book with line drawings as well.[1]

*Poems from Africa* was edited by Samuel Allen, who also wrote the introduction and translated some of the works that were included in the anthology. A poet himself, Allen was in Paris on the GI Bill at about the same time as Bearden. He first published his poetry in 1949 in *Présence Africaine,* a French literary journal founded by a group of West African writers and intellectuals who were promoting the Negritude movement, which included the idea of a distinctive black voice and style of expression in the arts. At the invitation of Richard Wright, Allen became the editor of the magazine's English content. During this time, he also translated into English, "Black Orpheus," an influential essay on African poetry of Negritude by Jean-Paul Sartre.

Bearden had met Allen while he was in the army, and they renewed their friendship in Paris. Together they were a part of a wider circle of American artists, writers, and musicians that included Wright, James Baldwin, Albert Murray, Herbert Gentry, Sidney Bechet, and Roy Eldridge, among others. Bearden already knew some of them from Harlem, but others were new acquaintances. As with Allen, several of those with whom he associated in Paris remained lifelong friends and collaborators.

1. Samuel Allen, ed., *Poems from Africa* (New York: Thomas Y. Crowell, 1973).

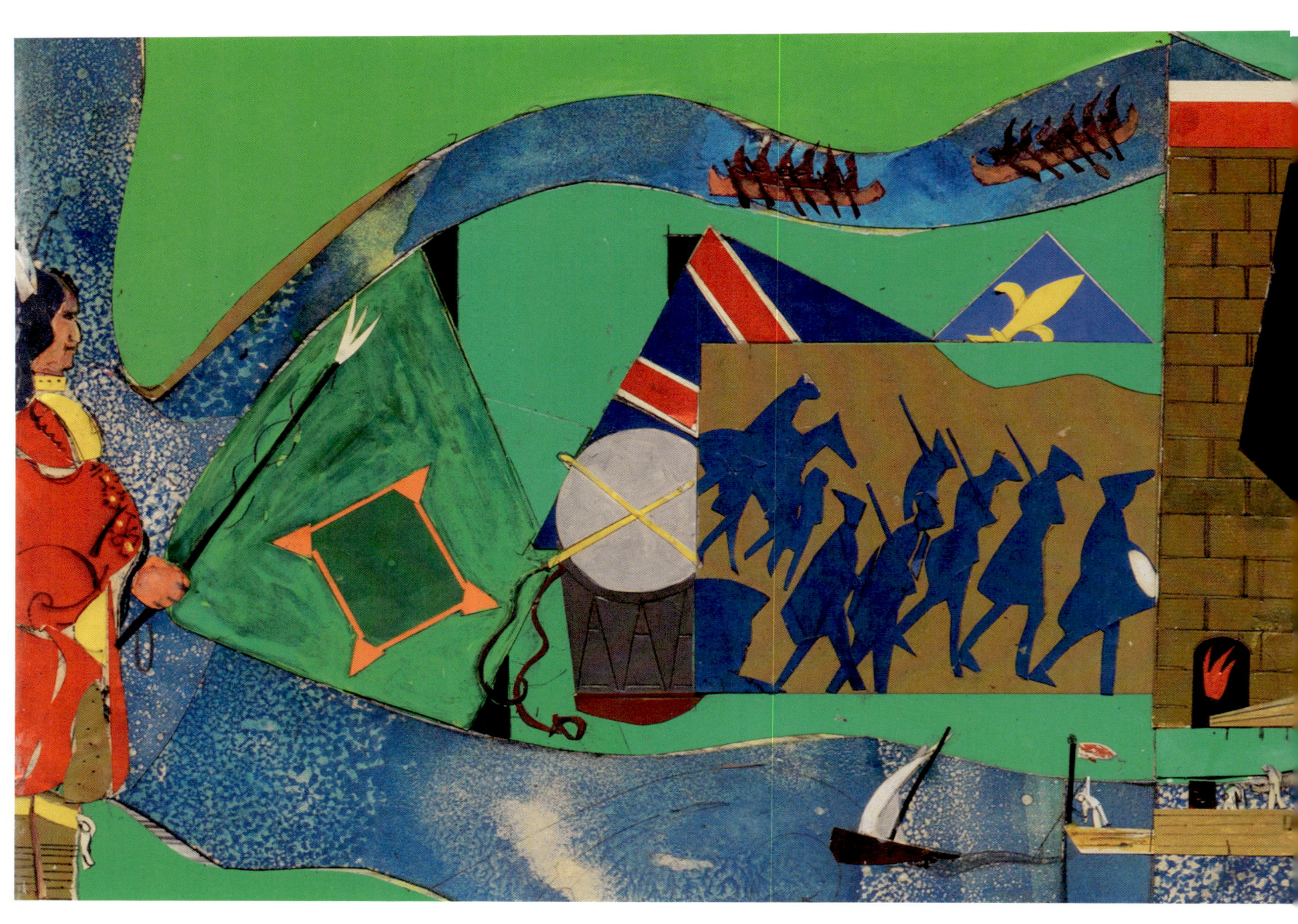



**PITTSBURGH RECOLLECTIONS**, 1984. COLLAGE ON FIBERBOARD, $10\frac{5}{8}$ X 50 INCHES

## GENEVA PRINT MAQUETTE, 1971 *(page 7)*

**THIS BOLDLY STYLIZED PANEL** is one of two closely related designs that Bearden created for a poster for an exhibition at the Rath Museum in Geneva, Switzerland, in 1971. *Eight Afro-American Artists* was the first show of its kind to be held in Europe. At the time, its organizer, Henry Ghent of the Brooklyn Museum, said that the intent was to "change a few stereotypes," adding that "we'd like them to know there are young blacks who are contemplative, who have the same esthetic concerns as artists everywhere."[1]

The design was one of Bearden's most distinctive. The version that was used for the Swiss exhibition poster was also made into a screenprint titled *Black in America*, which was published in an edition of fifty in 1976 as part of the Bicentennial. Another variant became the cover for *The Harvard Advocate, Special Issue, Black Odyssey: A Search for Home* in 1974.

1. Grace Glueck, "Art Notes," *The New York Times* (April 18, 1971).

## BLACK HISTORY, C.1979 *(pages 8/9)*

**WHILE THE PROJECT** for which this maquette was intended is unknown, it was possibly a mural for a school or university, as indicated by the globe and schoolhouse scene at center left.

Several of the motifs are distinctly Bearden. The profiled face at left and diagonal red stripes closely resemble the principal imagery of the poster that he designed for the exhibition of African American art in Geneva (see p. 7). He also used a variation in a large wall mural painted on a building on Martin Luther King Boulevard in downtown Atlanta in 1976.

The guitar player in a frontal pose at center appears in various guises in other collages, as does the procession of women at right. The group is, in fact, directly adapted from the religious ritual depicted in *Palm Sunday Procession*, a collage of 1967–68, which later became *Easter Procession* or *Processional*, a screenprint of 1983. Throughout his career, Bearden worked and reworked his visual ideas, creating an ever-expanding repertoire of images and motifs that invoke the ancestors and archetypes of African American history and culture.

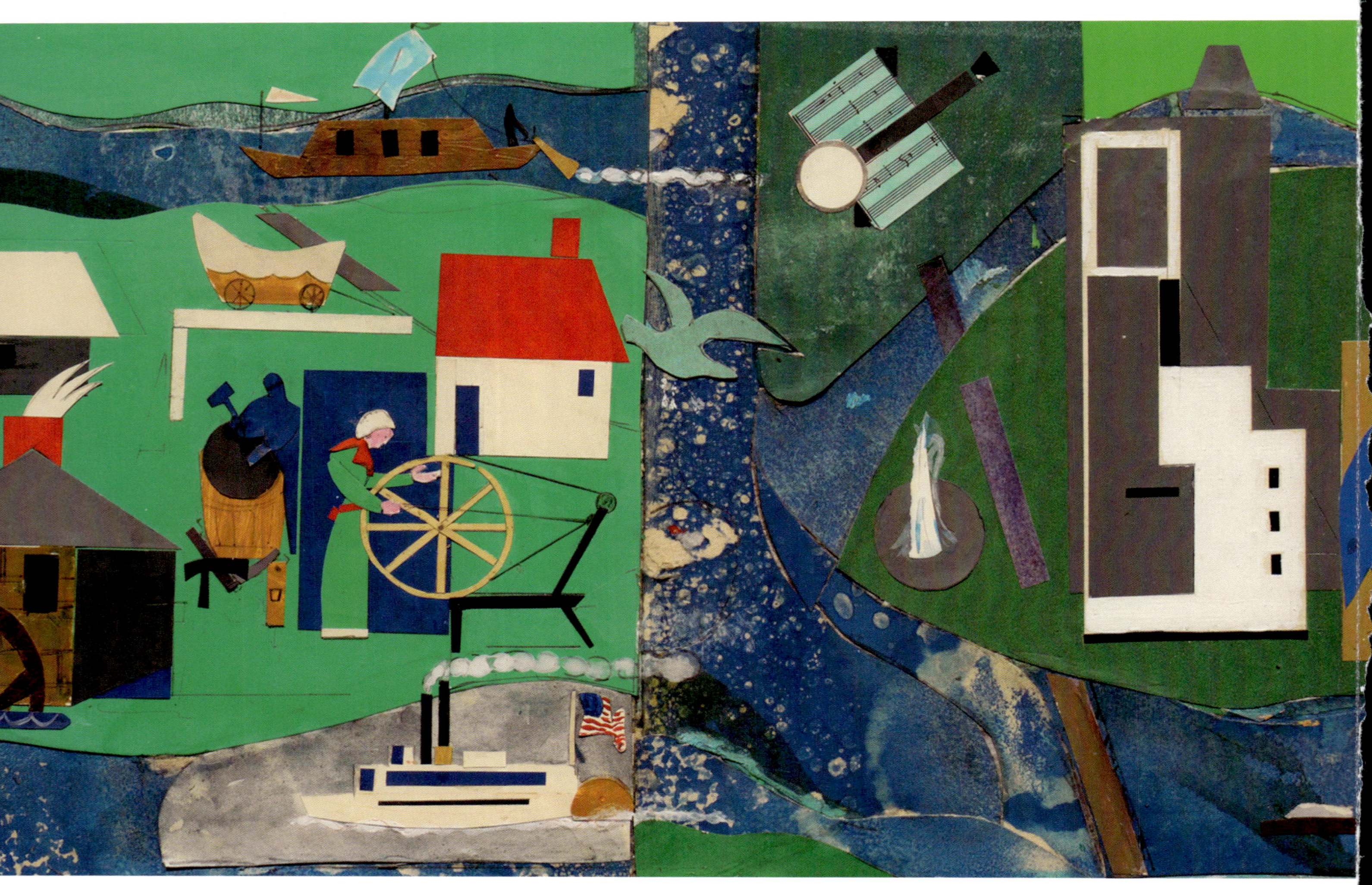

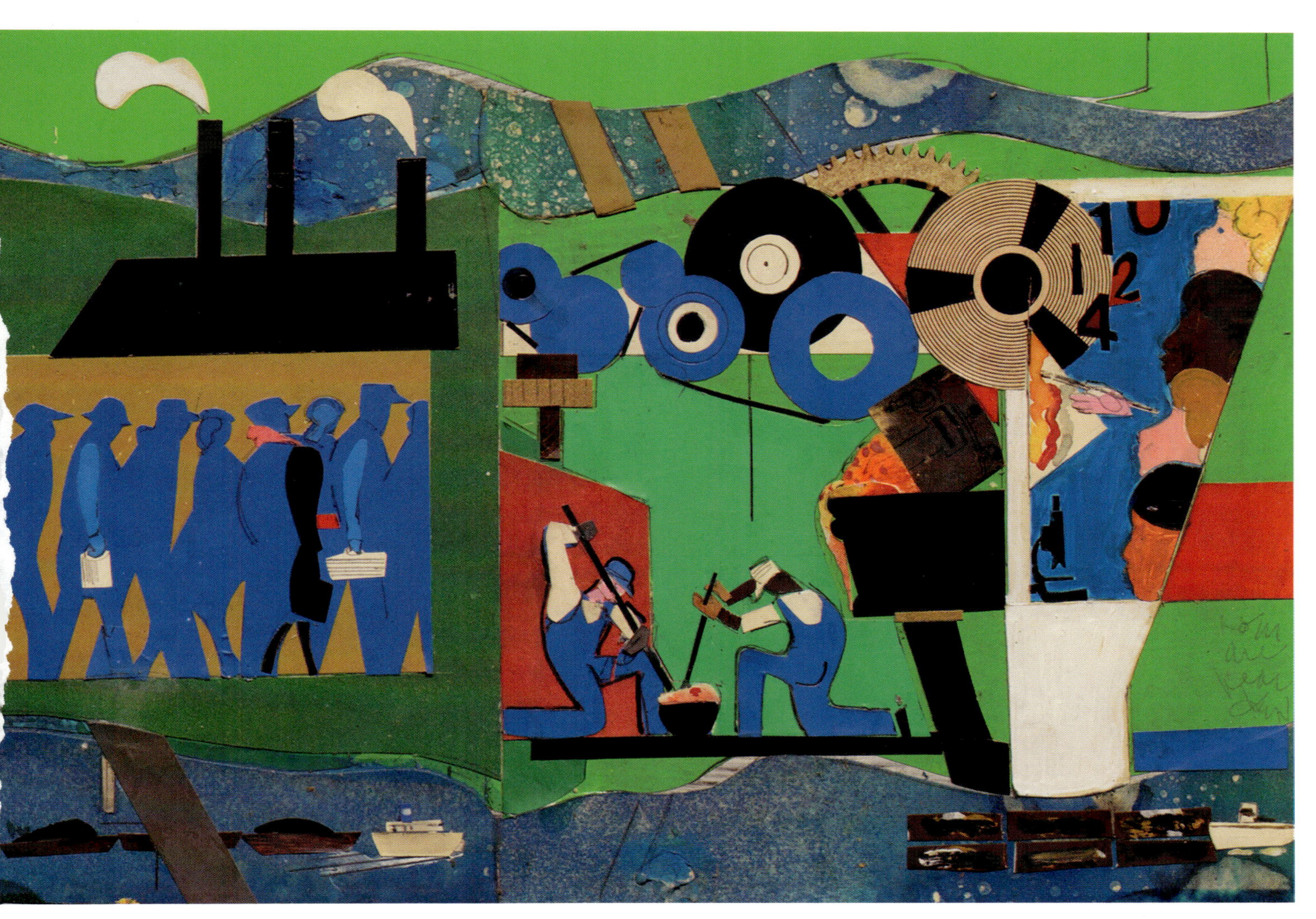

# PITTSBURGH RECOLLECTIONS, 1984

IN *PITTSBURGH RECOLLECTIONS*, Bearden presents a bold modernist narrative and historical panorama of a city that occupied an important place in his life and art.

The story begins at left with an image of one of the original inhabitants of the area at the meeting point of Pittsburgh's three rivers—the Allegheny, Monongahela, and Ohio—followed by references to Fort Pitt and the defeat of the French in the colonial era. Early industry is then represented by a waterwheel, forge, and spinning wheel, giving way to twentieth-century factory workers, smokestacks, gears and belts, and a crucible of molten steel, all symbols of the city's prosperity during that period. The final vignette at right looks to the future, with a microscope, discs, numbers, and four profiled faces that signify the economic shift to technology, education, and medical services that began with the collapse of the steel industry in the 1970s and early 1980s. Bearden also included a hand holding a paintbrush, a self-referential detail that further emphasizes the city's transition from its industrial past.

The design for *Pittsburgh Recollections* became a major subway mosaic that was installed at the downtown Gateway Center Station in 1984. Composed of 780 ceramic tiles from Bennington Potters in Vermont, it measures 13 x 60 feet. Recently appraised at $15 million, the mural is currently being dismantled, restored, and moved to a new location.

Bearden knew the city well, having spent some of his childhood there. When he was eight years old, he lived with his grandparents, Carrie and George Banks, who ran a boardinghouse in the steel-mill neighborhood of Lawrenceville. He returned in 1927 to finish high school, and one summer had a job on the night shift in a steel mill. *Pittsburgh Recollections* is one of a number of collages based on these experiences, from the early *Pittsburgh Memory* of 1964, to later works like *Mill Hand's Lunch Bucket* of 1978 and *Pittsburgh Memories* of 1983. In all, Bearden's Pittsburgh years provided a lifelong point of reference and a wealth of compelling images for his art.

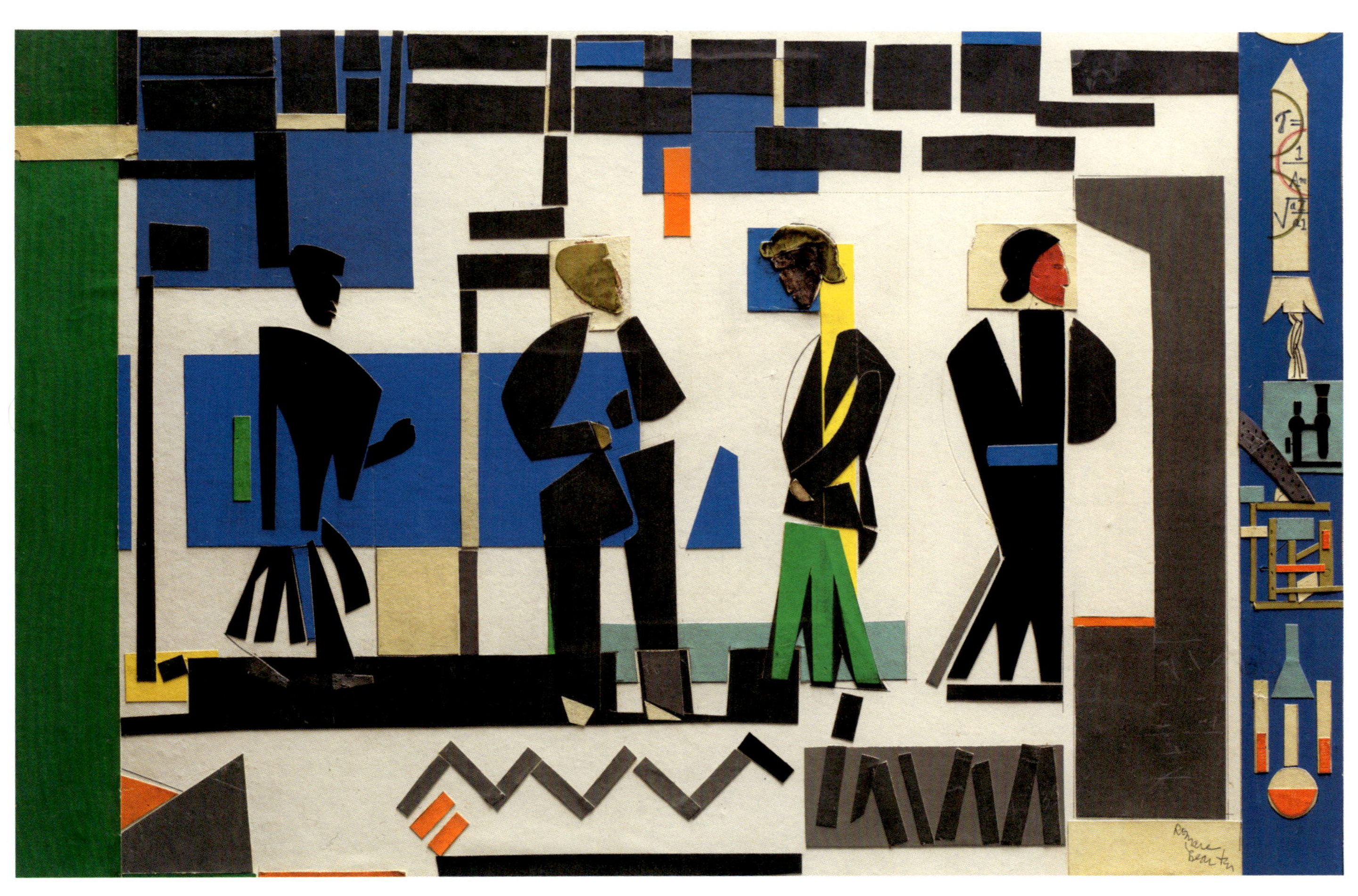

UNTITLED (*SCIENCE MAQUETTE*), c. 1973. COLLAGE ON FIBERBOARD, 13 X 20½ INCHES

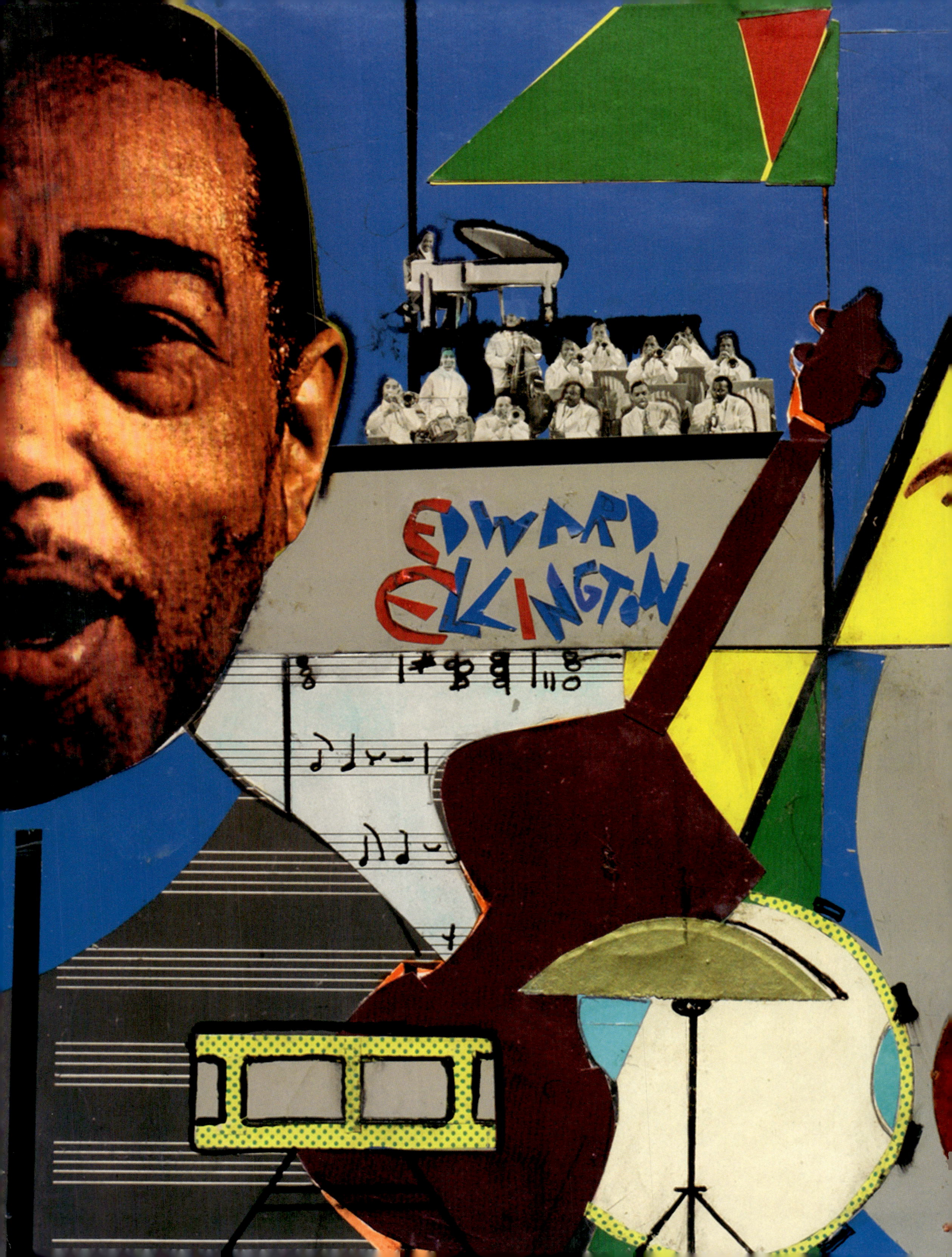

EDWARD ELLINGTON

# ROMARE BEARDEN



**BORN IN 1911 IN CHARLOTTE, NORTH CAROLINA,** Romare Howard Bearden moved with his family to New York City when he was three years old. After attending Lincoln University and Boston University, he graduated from New York University with a degree in education. He also studied drawing and painting with George Grosz at the Art Students League of New York, and in the 1930s and 1940s, became close friends with several older artists, including Stuart Davis, who was an important mentor.

In 1935, Bearden joined the Harlem Artists Guild and began contributing political cartoons to the weekly *Baltimore Afro-American.* From the mid-1930s through the 1960s, he was a caseworker with the New York City Department of Social Services, working on his art at night and on weekends.

Bearden's career as a painter was launched in 1940 with his first solo exhibition in Harlem. He had another solo show four years later at the G Place Gallery in Washington, DC, while he was serving in the Army. In 1945, shortly after his discharge, he joined the Kootz Gallery on 57th Street, and exhibited there for the next three years. He then traveled to Paris on the GI Bill in 1950, studying philosophy at the Sorbonne and visiting museums throughout France and Italy. Back home in Harlem, he married Nanette Rohan in 1954. Two years later, they moved to a loft on Canal Street.

After a few years painting abstractions in the late 1950s and early 1960s, Bearden turned to photomontage and collage, which established his reputation as a leading contemporary artist. He joined the Cordier & Ekstrom gallery in 1961, and was represented by them for the rest of his life. In 1963, Bearden, Hale Woodruff, Charles Alston, Norman Lewis, and others created Spiral, a group formed to promote the work of black artists and explore ways in which they could contribute to the ongoing Civil Rights movement. In a further expression of his lifelong commitment to the African American art community, he, Lewis, and Ernest Crichlow later established the Cinque Gallery, dedicated to supporting and exhibiting the work of emerging black artists.

Bearden was also a founding member of the Studio Museum in Harlem and the Black Academy of Arts and Letters. In 1964, he was appointed the first art director of the Harlem Cultural Council, a prominent African American advocacy group. He was elected to the American Academy of Arts and Letters in 1972.

Among his many publications are *A History of African American Artists: From 1792 to the Present,* coauthored with Harry Henderson and published posthumously in 1993; *Six Black Masters of American Art,* also coauthored with Harry Henderson (1972); and *The Painter's Mind: A Study of the Relations of Structure and Space in Painting,* coauthored with Carl Holty (1969).

Recognized as one of the most original visual artists of the twentieth century, Bearden has had a number of retrospectives, including those organized by the Museum of Modern Art (1971), Mint Museum of Art (1980), Detroit Institute of the Arts (1986), Studio Museum in Harlem (1991), and National Gallery of Art (2003). His work is represented in public collections across the country, such as the Metropolitan Museum of Art, Museum of Modern Art, Whitney Museum of American Art, National Gallery of Art, Philadelphia Museum of Art, Museum of Fine Arts, Boston, and Studio Museum in Harlem. In 1984, he received the Mayor's Award of Honor for Art and Culture in New York City, and in 1987, was awarded the prestigious President's National Medal of the Arts. He died in New York City in 1988.

*BESSIE, DUKE, AND LOUIS,* C.1981 (DETAIL). COLLAGE ON FIBERBOARD, 18 1/8 X 50 INCHES

# DC **MOORE** GALLERY

535 WEST 22ND STREET NEW YORK, NY 10011

212·247·2111 WWW.DCMOOREGALLERY.COM

Published on the occasion of the exhibition, *Romare Bearden: Idea to Realization*
DC Moore Gallery, February 3 – March 12, 2011

DC Moore Gallery represents The Romare Bearden Estate and The Romare
Bearden Foundation



ISBN: 978-0-9826316-5-2

Distributed by D.A.P./Distributed Art Publishers. 800.338.2665 or www.artbook.com

*Publications Manager: Kate Weinstein*
*Editing: SNAP Editions*
*Design: Joseph Guglietti with SNAP Editions*
*Principal Photography: © Bruce M. White*
*Printing: The Studley Press*

COVER: *Bessie, Duke, and Louis,* c. 1981 (detail). Collage on fiberboard, $18^{1}/_{8}$ x 50 inches
INSIDE COVER: *Pittsburgh Recollections,* 1984 (detail). Collage on fiberboard, $10^{5}/_{8}$ x 50 inches
PAGE 2: *Culture: Hartford Mural,* 1980 (detail). Collage on fiberboard, 18 x 12 inches
OPPOSITE: *A Symbolic Pageant of Afro-American History,* 1972 (detail). Collage on fiberboard, 6 x 26 inches